W9-DAC-648

INSIDE THE
NFL

JACKSONVILLE
JAGUARS

BY WILLIAM MEIER

SportsZone

An Imprint of Abdo Publishing
abdobooks.com

abdobooks.com

Published by Abdo Publishing, a division of ABDO, PO Box 398166, Minneapolis, Minnesota 55439. Copyright © 2020 by Abdo Consulting Group, Inc. International copyrights reserved in all countries. No part of this book may be reproduced in any form without written permission from the publisher. SportsZone™ is a trademark and logo of Abdo Publishing.

Printed in the United States of America, North Mankato, Minnesota
022019
092019

Cover Photo: Scott Halleran/Getty Images Sport/Getty Images
Interior Photos: Jamie Squire/Allsport/Getty Images Sport/Getty Images, 5; Allen Kee/ Getty Images Sport/Getty Images, 7; Michael S. Green/AP Images, 8, 21; Bryan Kelsen/ AP Images, 11; Scott Halleran/Getty Images Sport/Getty Images, 13; Felix Mizioznikov/ Shutterstock Images, 15; Al Messerschmidt/AP Images, 16; David J. Phillip/AP Images, 19; Al Behrman/AP Images, 22; Bill Frakes/Sports Illustrated/Getty Images, 25; Don Frazier/ AP Images, 27; Tony Gutierrez/AP Images, 29; Rick Wilson/The Florida Times-Union/AP Images, 31; Paul Spinelli/AP Images, 32, 35, 40; Scott Boehm/AP Images, 36

Editor: Patrick Donnelly
Series Designer: Craig Hinton

Library of Congress Control Number: 2018965342

Publisher's Cataloging-in-Publication Data

Names: Meier, William, author.
Title: Jacksonville Jaguars / by William Meier.
Description: Minneapolis, Minnesota : Abdo Publishing, 2020 | Series: Inside the NFL | Includes online resources and index.
Identifiers: ISBN 9781532118500 (lib. bdg.) | ISBN 9781532172687 (ebook)
Subjects: LCSH: Jacksonville Jaguars (Football team)--Juvenile literature. | National Football League--Juvenile literature. | Football teams--Juvenile literature. | American football--Juvenile literature.
Classification: DDC 796.33264--dc23

TABLE OF
CONTENTS

CHAPTER 1

MILE HIGH
SURPRISE

The Jacksonville Jaguars were playing in only their second season in the National Football League (NFL). They found themselves in an amazing, unlikely situation.

The Jaguars were leading the Denver Broncos 23–12 in the fourth quarter of a divisional playoff game on January 4, 1997. The crowd of 75,678 fans at Mile High Stadium in Denver had been stunned into silence. Their beloved Broncos had been favored to win the game by two touchdowns.

The Jaguars were an expansion franchise. That meant they had not been around long. In NFL history, no expansion team had played this well so quickly. Usually it takes new franchises many years before they can compete with the NFL's more established teams.

Mark Brunell led the Jaguars into hostile territory when they faced the Broncos in January 1997.

SURPRISE SUCCESS

Jacksonville went 4–12 in 1995. The Carolina Panthers also made their NFL debut that year. They finished 7–9. Previously, no NFL expansion team had won more than three games in its first season. The last time the NFL had added expansion teams was in 1976. The Tampa Bay Buccaneers finished 0–14 during that first season while the Seattle Seahawks went 2–12. The Jaguars and Panthers both reached conference championship games in their second seasons.

That success was partly due to free agency. A free agent is a player who has completed his contract and is free to sign with any team. Free agency fully started in the NFL in 1993. Before then, far fewer players switched teams. Jacksonville, for example, signed wide receiver Keenan McCardell after he had enjoyed some success with the Cleveland Browns. Once he was with the Jaguars, he became an even better player.

Jacksonville's team was made up mostly of players the other NFL teams did not want. Head coach Tom Coughlin had no experience in that role except at the college level.

Almost no one thought the Jaguars could win. Woody Paige, a columnist for the *Denver Post*, had written in that morning's newspaper, "Can we get a legitimate [real] team in here next Sunday?" He and many others assumed that the Broncos would

Jaguars running back Natrone Means dives for extra yards against Denver.

easily advance to the following week's American Football Conference (AFC) Championship Game.

But the Jaguars, behind quarterback Mark Brunell's clever passing and scrambling and Natrone Means's powerful but nimble running, had taken an 11-point lead. There were about 10 minutes left in the game. If the Jaguars could hold on, it would be one of the NFL's most shocking upsets ever.

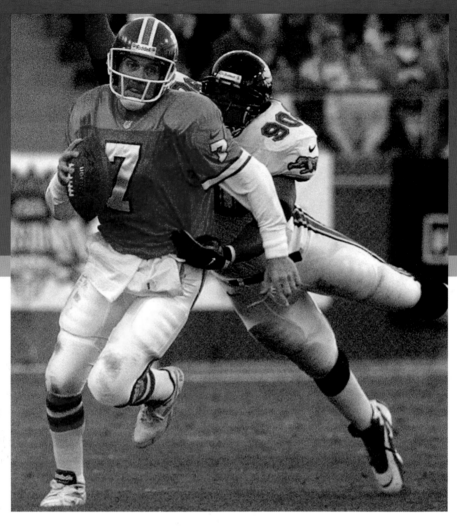

Jaguars defensive end Tony Brackens takes down Broncos quarterback John Elway during Jacksonville's 30–27 win.

Denver was not going to make it easy, though. The Broncos had star quarterback John Elway on their side, as well as many other talented offensive players. One of them, running back

Terrell Davis, scored on a 2-yard touchdown run. He then ran in a two-point conversion. That cut the Jaguars' lead to 23–20.

The pressure was back on Jacksonville. Mile High Stadium was one of the noisiest venues in the NFL. How would the Jaguars handle this difficult situation?

Very well, it turned out. Brunell led his offense 74 yards down the field in nine plays. On one of them, he scrambled for a 29-yard gain by dodging four Broncos. He finished the drive with a 16-yard touchdown pass to Jimmy Smith. The pass found Smith in the corner of the end zone, just out of a defender's reach. "All I had to do was hold my arms out," Smith said. "It was perfect." Jacksonville took a 30–20 lead with 3:39 left.

Denver scored a late touchdown, but it was not enough. Jacksonville had done what many thought was impossible. The Jaguars, in just their second season, had beaten the powerful Broncos 30–27. In the regular season, Denver had gone 13–3, tied for the best record in the NFL. Jacksonville had to win its final five games just to reach 9–7 and sneak into the playoffs.

"I'm sick to my stomach," Davis said after the game.

The Broncos wanted to get to the Super Bowl for Elway, whose impressive career was nearing its end. The Jaguars were

ROAD WARRIORS

Maybe the Jaguars' victory over Denver should not have been a complete surprise. After all, just the week before, they had defeated the Buffalo Bills, also 30–27, in a first-round playoff game. It was the Bills' first home playoff loss ever at Rich Stadium, where they had been 9–0. Before the Jaguars beat them, the Broncos had been 8–1 in all playoff games at Mile High Stadium.

hungry, too. Many of their players had been let go by other NFL teams. They were determined to show those teams that they had made a mistake. They proved that against the Broncos.

"People don't believe we're supposed to be here," said wide receiver Keenan McCardell, who had struggled before signing with Jacksonville in 1996. "But, hey, it don't matter, it don't matter."

Thanks to smart decisions in selecting coaches and players, the Jaguars had quickly become a good team. Amazingly, the next week Jacksonville found itself one step away from reaching the Super Bowl. It was not to be, however. The Jaguars lost 20–6 to the host New England Patriots in the AFC Championship Game.

The Jaguars, though, had proven that expansion teams did not need to wait long to compete with the NFL's best teams. In fact, Jacksonville would go on to reach the playoffs in the

✗ Jacksonville receiver Keenan McCardell hauls in a 31-yard touchdown pass in the January 1997 playoff game against Denver.

next three seasons, too. The team would also make the AFC Championship Game a second time after the 1999 season. The Jags fell short in that game, as well, losing 33–14 to the Tennessee Titans.

The Jaguars started strong in their first five seasons, but since then they have not won consistently. They have discovered, like many teams before them, that succeeding in the playoffs and reaching professional football's biggest game—the Super Bowl—is not easy.

CHAPTER 2

TOUCHDOWN JACKSONVILLE!

The Jaguars got off to a hot start, but that would not have happened if the NFL had not chosen to expand. And Jacksonville getting a team was no sure thing. In fact, the city in northern Florida was considered a long shot. The population in the Jacksonville area is not very big compared to other cities. Many thought that would hurt its chances.

Jacksonville's attempt to get an NFL team began on August 17, 1989. That was when the Touchdown Jacksonville! business partnership was formed. On September 16, 1991, Touchdown Jacksonville! filed an expansion application with the NFL. The application listed a nine-member group that included J. Wayne Weaver. He later would become the main owner of the Jaguars.

Jaguars fans have been vocal supporters of their team since 1995.

UP AND DOWN

Jimmy Smith overcame obstacles early in his career. Smith broke his leg and missed most of his rookie season with the Dallas Cowboys in 1992. The next year, he needed an emergency operation to remove his appendix. He also suffered through an infection and stomach problems. He did not play in 1994 after being released by Dallas and Philadelphia. In 1995, the Jaguars gave him a tryout after his mother sent head coach Tom Coughlin a binder filled with newspaper articles about her son. He became a five-time Pro Bowl selection with the Jaguars.

Touchdown Jacksonville! had received a commitment of $60 million from the Jacksonville City Council to fix up the Gator Bowl, the city's largest football stadium. In 1993, the NFL informed Touchdown Jacksonville! that additional renovations would be needed. At first, a solution could not be reached. Eventually, however, a new plan was agreed upon. The city would provide $53 million for renovations, and $68 million would come from team sources.

On October 26, 1993, the NFL announced that the existing team owners had unanimously voted for Charlotte, North Carolina, to receive the league's twenty-ninth team. That team became known as the Carolina Panthers. That left one more expansion team to be awarded. It became official on November 30, 1993. The Jacksonville Jaguars were named the league's thirtieth team. They would join the Panthers as new NFL teams in 1995.

✕ The Gator Bowl was significantly remodeled and renamed Municipal Stadium before the Jaguars' NFL debut in 1995.

On December 1, 1993, the *Florida Times-Union*, Jacksonville's daily newspaper, ran a front-page headline in huge type. It read "DO YOU BELIEVE IN MIRACLES? YES." That evening, thousands of fans celebrated at the Gator Bowl as season-ticket sales began. Within three weeks, the Jaguars had already sold more than 45,000 season tickets.

Clearly, Jacksonville was ready for some football. Now the Jaguars organization needed to get started on the hard work of building a team from scratch. As a successful businessman,

✕ The Jaguars valued offensive tackle Tony Boselli so much that they made him the second overall pick in the 1995 NFL Draft.

Weaver wanted to create a model football team and one that would contend for the playoffs right away.

One of Weaver's key moves was hiring Tom Coughlin as Jacksonville's coach and director of football operations in February 1994. Coughlin had been a successful head coach at Boston College but had no experience as an NFL head coach. However, he had served under the New York Giants' Bill Parcells as his wide receivers coach from 1988 to 1990. Coughlin, like his mentor, stressed discipline. He also was good at planning, and in Jacksonville he had time to do so.

Another important step was the NFL Expansion Draft on February 15, 1995. The other NFL teams were allowed to protect a certain number of players on their rosters. Then the Jaguars and Panthers took turns making picks from the rest. The Jaguars had the first choice and selected quarterback Steve Beuerlein. Jacksonville chose 31 players in all. A few, including Beuerlein, linebacker Keith Goganious, wide receiver Willie Jackson, and offensive guard Jeff Novak, became starters.

Probably even more important to Jacksonville was the 1995 NFL Draft. The Jaguars selected mammoth offensive tackle Tony Boselli, a former University of Southern California standout, with the number two pick. Boselli would be selected to five Pro Bowl teams in his seven years with the Jaguars.

Jacksonville did not just rely on the drafts to fill out its roster. In February 1995, the team signed free agent wide receiver Jimmy Smith, who had been out of the NFL in 1994. Also, on the day before the NFL Draft, the Jaguars traded the rights to their third- and fifth-round picks to the Green Bay Packers for quarterback Mark Brunell.

Through a variety of ways, Coughlin had built a talented roster. The Jaguars were now prepared for their debut season.

CHAPTER 3

"WHO ARE THESE GUYS?"

On September 3, 1995, the Jaguars played their first regular-season game at Jacksonville Municipal Stadium—the new name of the Gator Bowl stadium that had been almost completely renovated. In front of a crowd of 72,363, the Jaguars lost to the Houston Oilers 10–3.

Jacksonville had built a talented roster, but the team was young and inexperienced. It finished 4–12 in its first season. Still, many of the losses were close. Also, the Jaguars made an important discovery when Mark Brunell took over for Steve Beuerlein as the starting quarterback and excelled. In Green Bay, Brunell had been stuck on the bench behind star Brett Favre. But in Jacksonville, he finally had the opportunity to perform.

Offensive lineman Brian DeMarco celebrates Jacksonville's first win, a 17–16 victory over the Houston Oilers.

FRANCHISE FIRSTS

The Jaguars' first regular-season win came in their fifth game. They defeated the Oilers 17–16 in Houston on October 1, 1995. The next week, Jacksonville beat eventual AFC champion Pittsburgh 20–16 for its first home win. The Jaguars' other two victories in 1995 came against the Cleveland Browns.

The Jaguars added more talent before their second season. The team signed running back Natrone Means and wide receiver Keenan McCardell. Jacksonville also added some key players on defense. In the 1996 NFL Draft, the Jaguars took linebacker Kevin Hardy, defensive end Tony Brackens, and cornerback Aaron Beasley.

Jacksonville entered the 1996 season looking to build off its promising first year. The Jaguars got off to a shaky start, though, at 4–7. The turning point was a game on November 24 in Baltimore against the Ravens. Jacksonville trailed 25–10 in the fourth quarter. A loss would have meant that the Jaguars almost certainly would not make the playoffs. They did not quit, though. The Jaguars rallied to tie the score on two touchdown passes by Brunell. Then, in overtime, Mike Hollis made a 34-yard field goal to give Jacksonville a 28–25 win.

That victory demonstrated that the Jaguars were fighters. Jacksonville went on to win its final four regular-season games, too. Then the Jaguars made a remarkable playoff run,

Quarterback Mark Brunell blossomed when he got a chance to play in Jacksonville.

with victories at heavily favored Buffalo and Denver. Only in its second season in the NFL, the team got within one win of reaching the Super Bowl.

"I think the lack of respect is obvious," Brunell said a few days after the Jaguars' upset of the Broncos. "It's like, 'Who are these guys?' But I don't think that will happen anymore."

Fred Taylor breaks a tackle in a 1999 game against the Cincinnati Bengals. Taylor played in Jacksonville for 11 seasons.

On January 12, 1997, the Jaguars faced the Patriots in the AFC Championship Game. The Patriots' head coach was Tom Coughlin's mentor, Bill Parcells. Coughlin was stung by the 20–6 loss, but he knew his team's future looked bright.

Jacksonville got a scare before the next season even began when Brunell injured his knee in the preseason. But he was back by the third game of the regular season. The Jaguars and Steelers both finished the season 11–5, but a tiebreaker gave

Pittsburgh the AFC Central Division title. Jacksonville was a wild card. In the first round, the Jaguars went to Denver for a rematch of the previous season's historic playoff game. This time, the Broncos won easily, 42–17. Denver and John Elway would go on to win the Super Bowl.

"It was a monkey we had to get off our back," Broncos linebacker Bill Romanowski said about beating the Jaguars. "I thought about it [the loss the previous season] the whole game."

The defeat was disappointing, but Jacksonville had played another strong season. The Jaguars proved that their success the previous year was no fluke. But could they continue it?

Yes, they could. Jacksonville, with Coughlin guiding the way, had put together one of the NFL's most talented rosters, especially on offense. On April 18, 1998, Jacksonville added another piece to the puzzle, drafting running back Fred Taylor ninth overall. Taylor was a Florida native and a former star at the University of Florida. He was a natural fit with the Jaguars.

Jacksonville got off to a 5–0 start in 1998. One highlight was a 28–21 win over the visiting Miami Dolphins on October 12 on *Monday Night Football*. Taylor ran for a 77-yard touchdown.

WHAT AN ENDING!

Quarterback Mark Brunell's first game back from his knee injury in 1997 was Jacksonville's first *Monday Night Football* home game. It was Week 3 against Pittsburgh. Brunell threw for 306 yards, but the game wasn't decided until the last play. Jacksonville's Clyde Simmons blocked a 40-yard field-goal attempt and teammate Chris Hudson returned the ball 58 yards for a touchdown. The Jaguars won 30–21.

In his rookie season, he rushed for 1,223 yards and 14 touchdowns.

Brunell injured his ankle and missed the final three games of the regular season. But Jacksonville still finished 11–5 and easily won the AFC Central, its first division title. Brunell was back for the first round of the playoffs. The Jaguars, playing in their first home playoff game ever, beat the Patriots 25–10. Next up were the AFC East champion New York Jets.

Parcells was now coaching the Jets. He had left the Patriots after the 1996 season. And once again, he and his team were standing in the way of Coughlin and the Jaguars. The game was in chilly New York, and the Jets won 34–24. Brunell, playing on a left ankle that was still sore, struggled. He threw three interceptions. Coughlin was disappointed that the Jaguars turned the ball over four times.

✘ Tom Coughlin turned the expansion Jaguars into Super Bowl contenders.

For a third straight year, Jacksonville's season had ended in the playoffs. No NFL expansion team had ever made the playoffs in three of its first four seasons. Coughlin was not satisfied with that accomplishment, however. He went back to work and planned some more.

CHAPTER 4

BOOM,
THEN BUST

There is a saying in the NFL that defense wins titles. Tom Coughlin saw the wisdom in that philosophy and began to focus on improving his defense. Getting to the playoffs three seasons in a row had been great. Now, in 1999, he and the Jaguars wanted to win the Super Bowl.

In the Jaguars' 34–24 loss to the Jets in the 1998 playoffs, New York's Vinny Testaverde threw for 284 yards and Curtis Martin ran for 124. "You can't beat anybody with a defense like that," Coughlin said. "A game like that makes you think you might need to improve your defense."

Coughlin's first step toward doing that was to hire Dom Capers as defensive coordinator. Capers had been Carolina's head coach from 1995 through the 1998 season. He was

Jaguars cornerback Fernando Bryant picks off a pass in a 1999 preseason game against the Kansas City Chiefs.

MAKING THEIR POINTS

The Jaguars' 62–7 playoff win over the Dolphins in January 2000 was one of the biggest blowouts in playoff history. The 62 points and 55-point margin of victory both placed second in NFL playoff history. "It would have even been a bad game on PlayStation," Miami wide receiver Oronde Gadsden said. Only the Chicago Bears' 73–0 win over Washington in the 1940 NFL Championship Game was more lopsided.

known as an expert on defense. Continuing with the theme, Jacksonville used its first-round pick, twenty-sixth overall, in the 1999 NFL Draft on cornerback Fernando Bryant. The team also signed two key free agents, defensive tackle Gary Walker and safety Carnell Lake.

With a new emphasis on defense, Jacksonville appeared to have few weaknesses. More motivated than ever before, the Jaguars enjoyed their finest season in team history in 1999. They went an NFL-best 14–2 and won 11 straight games at one point. Their only losses were both to the Tennessee Titans. They lost 20–19 in Jacksonville in Week 3 and 41–14 in Tennessee in Week 16.

Was there anything the Jaguars could not do? Wide receiver Jimmy Smith had 116 catches for 1,636 yards. James Stewart and Fred Taylor teamed to rush for 19 touchdowns and more than 1,600 yards. The defense gave up an NFL-low 217 points.

Fred Taylor and the Jaguars dealt the Miami Dolphins a punishing playoff defeat in January 2000.

Jacksonville earned the number one seed in the AFC and a bye in the first round of the playoffs.

The unlucky second-round opponents were the Miami Dolphins. They never had a chance. The host Jaguars won 62–7 on January 15, 2000. The game was legendary Miami quarterback Dan Marino's last in a 17-season career. It also was Jimmy Johnson's final game as Dolphins coach. Taylor ran 90 yards for a touchdown in the first quarter, an NFL playoff record. Mark Brunell and backup quarterback Jay Fiedler each threw two touchdown passes. Smith had two touchdown catches. "It was a glorious day for football," Coughlin said.

It seemed as if nothing could stop Jacksonville from reaching its first Super Bowl. Unfortunately for the Jaguars, they had to face the Titans again in the AFC Championship Game. Tennessee had gone 13–3 and finished second to Jacksonville in the AFC Central.

Jacksonville led 14–10 at halftime of the conference title game. However, visiting Tennessee scored 23 unanswered points in the second half and won 33–14 to crush the Jaguars' Super Bowl dreams. Titans quarterback Steve McNair passed for just 112 yards, but he ran for 91 yards and two touchdowns. Brunell threw for a score but was intercepted twice. He also lost a fumble. In a sloppy game, the Jaguars had six turnovers and the Titans four.

Jacksonville had gone 15–0 against the rest of the NFL during the 1999 regular season and postseason. Against the Titans, the Jaguars finished 0–3. "For whatever reason, we

Hardy Nickerson was a five-time Pro Bowl linebacker who arrived from Tampa Bay after the 1999 season.

didn't play as well as we anticipated we would," Coughlin said. "It's a bitter pill to swallow."

The loss would mark the end of an era for Jacksonville. The expansion team that had done so well putting together a talented group of players would not be able to keep all of them over the next few seasons.

The NFL started using a salary cap in 1994. Under this system, the amount of money a team can spend on player salaries is limited. The Jaguars had given big contracts to

Defensive tackle Marcus Stroud was one of the few bright spots for Jacksonville during the early 2000s.

several players during the previous several years. To stay within the salary-cap rules, they now had to start letting go of many star players. That affected the team's success on the field.

Injuries also hampered the Jaguars. Offensive tackle Leon Searcy hurt his knee before the 2000 season and never played again in the NFL. Carnell Lake missed all of 2000 with an ailing foot. Jacksonville went 7–9 in 2000 and missed the playoffs for the first time since 1995.

The next two seasons, 2001 and 2002, were also frustrating. The Jaguars ran into more salary problems. As a result, they had to release numerous veterans including Keenan McCardell,

Lake, and linebacker Hardy Nickerson. They even made Tony Boselli, one of the most popular players in team history, available in the 2002 Expansion Draft. The NFL's newest team, the Houston Texans, chose Boselli with the first pick, though rather than play for the Texans he retired because of injuries.

Jacksonville went 6–10 in both 2001 and 2002. The team was able to add some talented players, including defensive tackles Marcus Stroud and John Henderson, through the NFL Draft.

J. Wayne Weaver, the Jaguars' owner, decided that it was time to rebuild the team. On December 30, 2002, he fired Coughlin, who had been the only head coach in team history. Weaver said it was a tough decision, but he believed that the team needed to "move in a new direction."

Coughlin had gone 72–64, including 4–4 in the playoffs, with Jacksonville. He later became the New York Giants' head coach and led them two Super Bowl titles.

CHAPTER 5

A CONSTANT CHANGE

The hiring of Jacksonville's second head coach was a big deal. Tom Coughlin had been with the Jaguars almost from the first day that they had been in the NFL.

Who would J. Wayne Weaver choose as Coughlin's replacement? He picked someone who was very different from Coughlin. On January 16, 2003, the team hired Jack Del Rio as its next head coach.

Del Rio had been Carolina's defensive coordinator in 2002. In his one year with the Panthers, their defense made a dramatic improvement in yards allowed. They went from thirty-first—which was last in the NFL—to second.

When the Jaguars hired him, Del Rio was 39 years old—young for an NFL head coach. He had played 11 seasons as a

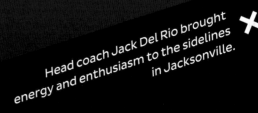

Head coach Jack Del Rio brought energy and enthusiasm to the sidelines in Jacksonville.

✕ Byron Leftwich brought his big arm and leadership abilities to Jacksonville in 2003.

linebacker in the NFL. Del Rio was considered a "players coach." He rarely screamed at his players, unlike Coughlin.

The Jaguars continued to rebuild over the next several months. In 2003, the team hired Baltimore Ravens executive James Harris to make roster decisions. Then, on April 26, Jacksonville selected quarterback Byron Leftwich with the seventh pick in the NFL Draft. He was viewed as Mark Brunell's replacement in the future. And that future arrived quickly. Brunell injured his throwing elbow early in the 2003 season and was out for the year. Leftwich passed for 14 touchdowns in

13 starts. He got help from Fred Taylor, who set a career high with 1,572 rushing yards. But the Jaguars finished only 5–11. They still had a ways to go.

In March 2004, Jacksonville traded Brunell to Washington. More responsibility was put on the broad shoulders of the 6-foot-5, 250-pound Leftwich. He handled it just fine. The Jaguars finished 9–7 and barely missed the playoffs.

Jacksonville headed into the 2005 season with plenty of optimism. The Jaguars' defense had become very strong, especially in the middle of the defensive line with Marcus Stroud and John Henderson. Leftwich injured an ankle in Week 12 at Arizona, but backup David Garrard stepped in and led Jacksonville to four wins in the final five regular-season games. The Jaguars went 12–4 , earning a wild-card berth in the AFC Playoffs.

The Jaguars had made their first playoff appearance since the 1999 season. But their 28–3 loss to New England in the first round showed that they needed to improve their offense. They selected promising running back Maurice Jones-Drew with their second-round pick in the 2006 NFL Draft.

Jacksonville still went into the 2006 season with high hopes. But Leftwich suffered a season-ending injury. Jones-Drew was a bright spot. He averaged an AFC-best 5.7 yards per carry and rushed for 13 touchdowns.

On August 31, 2007, the Jaguars surprised many people when they released Leftwich and announced that they were going with Garrard as their starting quarterback. The move worked. Garrard went 9–3 in the 12 games he started. He missed the other four with injuries. Taylor ran for 1,202 yards, and Jones-Drew finished with 768 rushing yards. Taylor made his first Pro Bowl. Jacksonville finished 11–5 and earned another wild-card playoff berth.

Jacksonville traveled to Pittsburgh for the first round of the 2007 playoffs. Jones-Drew scored two touchdowns, one on the ground and the other through the air. An interception return for a score by Rashean Mathis also helped. Entering the fourth quarter, the Jaguars led 28–10.

But the Steelers rallied for three quick touchdowns and took a 29–28 lead on Najeh Davenport's 1-yard run with 6:21 left. Garrard then made the game's key play, running 32 yards on fourth-and-two to Pittsburgh's 11-yard line with 1:56 remaining. His scamper set up Josh Scobee's game-winning 25-yard field goal with 37 seconds left.

An even harder task awaited in the second round of the playoffs. Jacksonville had to play at New England. The Patriots were the first team in league history to finish the regular season 16–0. The Jaguars put up a fight. Garrard threw two touchdown passes, and the score was tied 14–14 at halftime. Quarterback Tom Brady and the Patriots were playing too well, however. Brady went 26-for-28, setting an NFL record for completion percentage in any playoff or regular-season game at 92.9. For the second time in three years, the Patriots ended the Jaguars' season, this time by a score of 31–20.

Jones-Drew, now the team's main running back, rushed for 1,391 yards and 15 touchdowns in 2009, but Jacksonville lost its final four games to finish 7–9, then went 8–8 in 2010. Over the next few years, the front office attempted to make the team better with high draft picks such as quarterback Blaine Gabbert (tenth overall pick in 2011) and wide receiver Justin Blackmon (fifth overall pick in 2012). Unfortunately for the Jaguars,

FRED TAYLOR

Fred Taylor was one of the original great Jacksonville players. He grew up in Pahokee, Florida, and played college football with the hometown Florida Gators. Taylor went on to have a 13-year career in the NFL. He played 11 seasons with the Jaguars and finished with 11,695 rushing yards for his career. Through the 2018 season, Taylor held dozens of team records for rushing.

X Pro Bowl cornerback Jalen Ramsey breaks up a pass intended for Antonio Brown in the Jaguars' playoff upset of the Steelers in January 2018.

neither player lived up to the high expectations put on them. Del Rio was fired during the 2011 season.

Shortly after Del Rio left, Weaver decided to sell the team to Pakistani-American businessman Shahid Khan, who also owned a soccer club in England's Premier League. The team finished under .500 in each season from 2011 to 2016. Crowds in Jacksonville began to dwindle as the performance on the field went downhill, and talk of moving the team to London, England, began to pick up steam.

But things turned around in early 2017. The organization brought Coughlin back to serve as executive vice president of football operations. He and new head coach Doug Marrone helped the Jaguars make a quick turnaround. Led by a strong defense that included young cornerback Jalen Ramsey and defensive end Calais Campbell, the Jaguars went 10–6 and made it back to the postseason.

The Jaguars opened the playoffs at home with a 10–3 win over Buffalo. The next week, Jacksonville went to Pittsburgh and pulled off a huge upset. Rookie running back Leonard Fournette rushed for 109 yards and three touchdowns and the Jaguars won a 45–42 shootout. They were now back in the AFC Championship Game for the first time in 18 years.

The Jaguars had to go back to New England and play the defending Super Bowl champion Patriots. Jaguars quarterback Blake Bortles threw for 293 yards and Jacksonville led by 10 in the fourth quarter. But Brady led two late touchdown drives for the Patriots, who came back to win 24–20.

Despite a disappointing 5–11 showing in 2018, Jacksonville fans had good things to look forward to under Marrone and Coughlin and reason to hope the Jaguars were back to their winning ways.

TIMELINE

The Touchdown Jacksonville! partnership is formed to lead the community effort to attract an NFL franchise.

1989

Armed with a $60 million commitment from Jacksonville City Council to renovate the Gator Bowl, Touchdown Jacksonville! files an expansion application with the NFL.

1991

The NFL announces that Jacksonville has been awarded an NFL franchise.

1993

On February 21, the Jaguars hire Tom Coughlin of Boston College as head coach and director of football operations.

1994

The Jaguars lose 10–3 in their inaugural game against the Houston Oilers on September 3.

1995

The Jaguars shock the Denver Broncos in the playoffs on January 4 before losing to the New England Patriots in the AFC Championship Game on January 12.

1997

The Jaguars select running back Fred Taylor with the ninth pick of the NFL Draft. Taylor will become Jacksonville's all-time leading rusher.

1998

Playing in their first home playoff game, the Jaguars top New England 25–10 on January 3. The Jaguars lose 34–24 to the host New York Jets in the second round.

1999

The Jaguars finish an NFL-best 14–2 in the regular season but fall short of the Super Bowl after losing to the visiting Tennessee Titans in the AFC Championship Game.

1999

Jacksonville fires Coughlin as coach and direction of football operations on December 30.

2002

On January 16, the Jaguars hire Jack Del Rio as coach. On April 26, Jacksonville selects quarterback Byron Leftwich with the seventh overall pick in the NFL Draft.

2003

The Jaguars go 12–4 in the regular season and make their first playoff appearance in six seasons.

2005

Jimmy Smith, the franchise's all-time leading receiver, announces his retirement on May 11.

2006

Jacksonville releases Taylor on February 16. In 11 seasons with the team, he rushed for 11,271 yards.

2009

Del Rio is fired, and Weaver sells the Jaguars to businessman Shahid Khan.

2011

Coughlin is brought back to work in the team's front office. Doug Marrone takes over as head coach and leads the Jaguars to the AFC Championship Game.

Despite another strong defensive showing, the Jaguars struggle on offense and finish 5–11.

The Jaguars use the third pick in the draft to select quarterback Blake Bortles from Central Florida.

Linebacker Paul Posluszny leads the NFL with 122 solo tackles but the Jaguars go 4–12.

Mike Mularkey is hired as head coach but lasts just one year and is fired after a 2–14 season.

2012

2013

2014

2017

2018

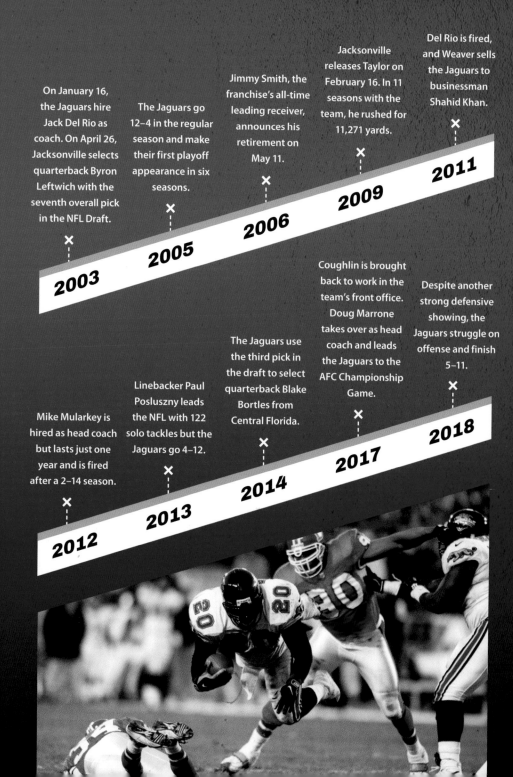

QUICK STATS

FRANCHISE HISTORY

1995–

SUPER BOWLS

None

AFC CHAMPIONSHIP GAMES

1996, 1999, 2017

DIVISION CHAMPIONSHIPS

1998, 1999, 2017

PLAYOFF APPEARANCES

1996, 1997, 1998, 1999, 2005, 2007, 2017

KEY COACHES

Tom Coughlin (1995–2002): 68–60, 4–4 (playoffs)
Jack Del Rio (2003–11): 68–71, 1–2 (playoffs)

KEY PLAYERS
(position, seasons with team)

Tony Boselli (OT, 1995–2001)
Tony Brackens (DE, 1996–2003)
Mark Brunell (QB, 1995–2003)
Calais Campbell (DE, 2017–)
Donovin Darius (S, 1998–2006)
David Garrard (QB, 2002–10)
John Henderson (DT, 2002–09)
Maurice Jones-Drew (RB, 2006–13)
Byron Leftwich (QB, 2003–06)
Rashean Mathis (CB, 2003–12)
Keenan McCardell (WR, 1996–2001)
Jalen Ramsey (CB, 2016–)
Allen Robinson (WR, 2014–17)
Josh Scobee (K, 2004–14)
Jimmy Smith (WR, 1995–2005)
Marcus Stroud (DT, 2001–07)
Fred Taylor (RB, 1998–2008)

HOME FIELDS

TIAA Bank Field (1995–)
Also known as Alltel Stadium, Jacksonville Municipal Stadium, EverBank Field

*All statistics through 2018 season

QUOTES AND ANECDOTES

The Touchdown Jacksonville! business partnership was confident its city would get an NFL team. In fact, it had gone ahead and selected the team name, Jaguars, in a fan contest in 1991. The Sharks, Stingrays, and Panthers were other finalists.

When the Jacksonville Jaguars started playing in the NFL in 1995, it gave Florida three NFL teams: the Jaguars, the Miami Dolphins, and the Tampa Bay Buccaneers. Florida became the third state with three teams. California had the Oakland Raiders, San Diego Chargers, and San Francisco 49ers, and New York had the Buffalo Bills, New York Giants, and New York Jets. California gained a fourth team when the Rams moved from St. Louis back to Los Angeles before the 2016 season but returned to three teams when the Raiders moved to Las Vegas.

Jacksonville fans were thrilled by their team's stunning 30–27 upset of the Denver Broncos in the second round of the 1996 playoffs. To welcome their heroes home, 40,000 Jaguars fans waited until 1:30 a.m. to greet the team plane at the Jacksonville airport.

In 1998, Jacksonville-area McDonald's restaurants offered the "Boselli Burger" in honor of popular Jaguars offensive lineman Tony Boselli. The burger featured three hamburger patties with lettuce and tomatoes.

In 2014, the Jaguars were struggling to get fans to come to games. So they decided to be creative. The team added two hot tubs in the upper deck of the stadium. Fans can purchase tickets to sit outside the spa and also enjoy floating in one of the tubs during the game.

GLOSSARY

contend
Compete for a title or a prize.

contract
An agreement to play for a certain team.

discipline
Activity, exercise, or a regimen that develops or improves a skill.

draft
A system that allows teams to acquire new players coming into a league.

expansion
The addition of new teams to increase the size of a league.

franchise
A sports organization, including the top-level team and all minor league affiliates.

legend
A person who achieves a high level of fame.

lopsided
Uneven; unequal.

mentor
A person who helps teach and tutor a less experienced person.

nimble
Quick and light movement; able to move with ease.

rookie
A professional athlete in his or her first year of competition.

venue
The scene or setting in which something takes place.

MORE INFORMATION

BOOKS

Graves, Will. *NFL's Top 10 Upsets*. Minneapolis, MN: Abdo Publishing, 2018.

Karras, Steven M. *Jacksonville Jaguars*. New York: AV2 by Weigl, 2018.

Kortemeier, Todd. *Jacksonville Jaguars*. Minneapolis, MN: Abdo Publishing, 2017.

ONLINE RESOURCES

Booklinks
NONFICTION NETWORK
FREE! ONLINE NONFICTION RESOURCES

To learn more about the Jacksonville Jaguars, visit **abdobooklinks.com** or scan this QR code. These links are routinely monitored and updated to provide the most current information available.

PLACES TO VISIT

Pro Football Hall of Fame
2121 George Halas Dr. NW
Canton, OH 44708
330–456–8207
profootballhof.com

This hall of fame and museum highlights the greatest players and moments in the history of the NFL.

TIAA Bank Field
1 TIAA Bank Field Dr.
Jacksonville, FL 32202
904–633–2000
jaguars.com/stadium

The Jacksonville Jaguars' home stadium since the team began in the 1990s.

INDEX

ABOUT THE AUTHOR

William Meier has worked as an author and editor in the publishing industry for more than 25 years. He resides in St. Louis, Missouri, with his wife and their poodle, Macy.